In the Name of Allah the Compassionate the Merciful

بِسْمِ ٱللهِ ٱلرَّحْمَٰنِ ٱلرَّحِيم

I would like to give a special thanks to WF-Aid who took their time to get pictures from the children in Syria for this book and will be the organization that takes all funds from this book toward those in need in Syria. A huge thanks to my mother in-law, Cynthia McCabe for all the time she put into doing the illustrations for this project. And another huge thanks to sr.Zahra for helping make this book more realistic with all your efforts to help make this book much more better. The greatest thanks to Allah swt who has given me the opportunity to do just this little for those in need. May Allah swt bless all of you that have supported this cause throughout!

Ameen.

Please recite surah al Fatiha for the Imam of our Time, Imam al Mahdi atfs

14 June 2011

Dear Diary,

I can't believe it! I'm turning nine today. Mom gave me this Diary to write in it as she says I am getting older and may need it, not sure what that means but at least I get to draw in it too. My Mom said she had one too when she was younger, so she thought it was a perfect starter gift for my ninth birthday.

I guess the most appropriate thing to do is to tell you a little about myself. My name is Maryam, I live in Syria with my parents and sister Layla who is four. Mom and Dad told me I'm going to have an amazing birthday party because today marks me becoming of age in Islam too. I'm excited because this means I'm getting older, but I'm also secretly scared because now all those duties are on me like praying and fasting. Do you think I'm going to be able to please Allah? If you think I can, then I feel more confident that I will be able too.

Anyways, so I am going to enjoy eating yummy cake and opening all my birthday gifts. I think I know what Mom got me, I think it's an aqeeq ring and a prayer outfit. I can't wait to see all my beautiful gifts. I hope no one got me a doll this year because I'm too old for that. I'm going to wear my pretty purple dress and the matching hijab that sparkles. Mom put the decorations up and has been cleaning all day because a lot of my family members are coming over for my birthday. Fatima and I always play when she comes over, she's my cousin and best friend. Everyone tells us we look alike and some have even said we look like twins! I enjoy doing art with her, I think she is a better artist than myself but it's fun drawing and coloring anyways. In fact to show you my art talent I will sketch you a picture after my birthday ok?

Oh mom just called me for my first prayer that is going to be recorded for a good deed. Write later.

Sincerly,

Maryam

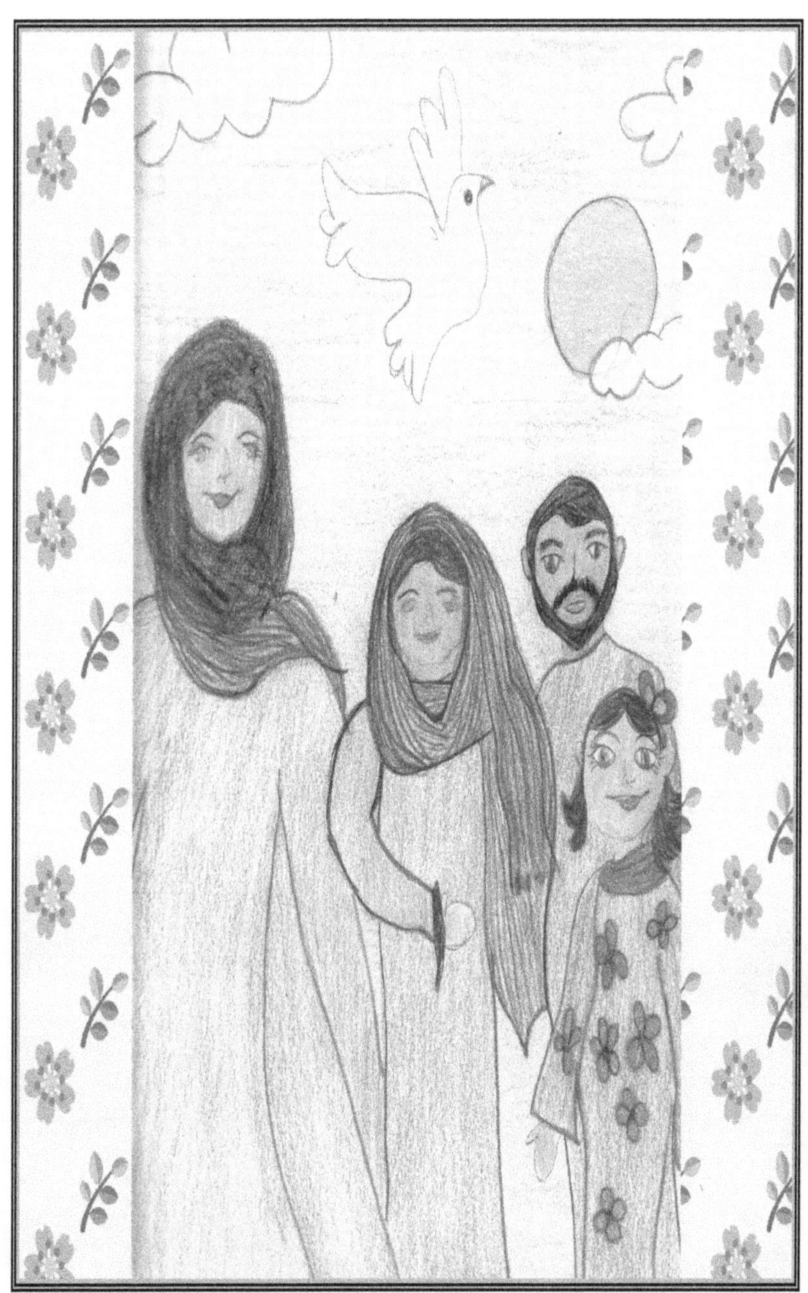

15 June 2011

Dear Diary,

Oh no! You aren't going to believe this but as I ended my birthday the protesters started such a loud riot. I thought we would be shot as they marched and chanted past our house. There is so much chaos going on outside. I wondered if a war would break out right then and there as I saw several people get shot at. I heard sirens roaring through the smokey air. The people were all over yelling and some were crying. What's going to happen? I hear Mom and Dad say they are worried for my sister Layla and mines safety.

My birthday had gone so perfectly. I did get that aqeeq ring and prayer outfit from my Mom. I also got a set of sketch papers and really cool sketch pens. I will draw you a picture when I have more light. Right now I lay in bed under my blankets next to Fatima as she spent the night at my house. We are in my room with the lights off and I'm using my little flashlight writing because writing to you dear Diary is calming me down.

I'm scared, will we be ok? It's so hard to even concentrate on writing to you because of all the noise outside my bedroom window.

I can hear Mom and Dad talking about what they should do. My Dad has told my Mom he is worried to go to work tomorrow, but he has to. I hear Mom telling Dad that we will be ok when he's gone and that she will invite my auntie over tomorrow for the day so we can be together and not alone.

Sorry I got to go Dad is telling me to shut the flashlight off.

P.s. If I don't get to write to you again just know I did not make the riot, pray for me.

Maryam

July 2, 2011

Dear Diary,

Sorry it has taken me so long to write. This is the longest I have gone in not writing to you. After my last letter to you I tucked you under the bed and had forgotten all about writing. There has been so much hate and anger causing all these riots, I don't even know how many people I have seen get shot at in front of my eyes. Dad got worried for us every day as he left for work, so we had to move into our grandparents place. It already had my uncle, auntie and our five cousins living there. We are being squished into this little house but I know Dad just wants us to be safe and he worries to much about us already. The good part is Fatima and I get to play everyday after school. I really love my family and friends, please pray that all this anger to stop and we can go back to living a normal life like before. I miss my room and the smell of Dad's old chair as I sat next to him he would read me so many interesting stories. I miss our house. I can not wait to go back.

Pray for us, I just want my life back. Got to go to bed as morning prayers are not to far away.

Maryam

July 31, 2011

Dear Diary,

Today is my first day fasting since I became of age. This is exciting because Mom and Dad told me that if I work hard and fasted everyday I will get a special gift at Eid. Between you and I, I'll tell you a secret, I love to fast. I know it's hard work but I get to wake up early and spend time alone with Mom and Dad but also at night too. I feel included in the fun eating special meals and yummy treats. I get to help Mom and aunt make supper tonight. We will be eating yummy rice and kabab. She always makes yummy dessert for us to enjoy after dinner, which tonight we are going to have baklava. I will help them with the soup by cutting up the veggies and also by helping make sure nothing boils over. Fatima doesn't like cooking much so she got out of helping in the kitchen by saying she will wash the clothes and hang them out to dry.

I love Ramadan everyone gets together and we enjoy listening to Quran which Dad recites. I sit on his lap tentatively listening. What is going to be really fun this year is we are living with grandma and grandpa. Grandma always sneaks me tea in the morning before we eat and it always has lots of delicious sugar. Even though living in this house is a little squishy it's a lot of fun too.

Got to put my pen down I'm a little tired but I'll draw you a picture at the end. Have a happy Ramadan dear Diary.

Maryam

RAMADAN

September 6, 2011

Dear Diary,

My Dad was just shot! I can not believe it, isn't it enough we have lost our home! What did we do wrong? Why are we being put in this situation? Why have they shot my father? I didn't do anything wrong, I swear to God I didn't do anything wrong dear Diary. My Mom is crying all day, my grandparents are trying to console her but her screams are ringing in my ears. I watched her fall to her knees at my father's body which laid motionless on the dirty ground outside. The blood wouldn't stop coming out of the bullet wound. A man grabbed my father and ran him to the hospital, "it was too late" one of the doctors said as my mother screamed again. She just kept yelling over and over

"Why?" I don't know why. I don't know what we are going to do. I mean really I am only nine, what can I do? I need to go, I just can't bare to write anymore.

I miss my dad so much already. I miss him Diary, I really miss him.

Maryam

September 28, 2011

Dear Diary,

Again I have left off writing to you for some time. Really it's not my fault actually. I keep meaning to come home after school to write but then another riot breaks out and we are held at school for sometime. We got a phone call today to say that there had been a huge riot, people were setting things on fire. It was a devastating phone call as Mom was told my cousins along with my grandparents, uncle and auntie had been killed in the riot. And there were several other people who did not make it either. We are alone now, I'm very scared to be honest but I need to be brave for my Mom and Layla. I miss Fatima so much, I miss everyone. I can't believe what our home has turned into. It's hard to even write these words because it seems not real. I don't even understand why it has all happened. My mom keeps telling me that I'm too young to know all that is going on in the world and she cries telling me that my sister and I should have never seen such things at such a young age.

I miss my family, my dad, my grandparents and all the rest we lost. Please pray for them dear Diary that they have ease in the grave now. I wonder, when will this hate end? I just want peace, I want my home back and I want our big happy family back. I want to go back to my ninth birthday when everyone was happy and cheerful. I know this would never be possible. I really don't know what to do. My Mom has told me she is worried about me too much so she is not allowing me to go to school anymore. I keep asking Allah "what did I do wrong?" My Mom has told me so many times that this is just a test, but I don't think I was very good at tests in school. Mom tells me I have to keep strong and to remember that Allah is the best of planners. I pray every prayer and I do it from the bottom of my heart because then I know Allah will be happy with us and He will help us out of these horrible fights and so much hate.

Got to go.

Your sad and secretly broken,

Maryam

October 2, 2011

Dear Diary,

I have a secret, but don't tell anyone! My Mom told me to pack my school bag up with my clothes because we are going to spend the night away from home. I don't know where we are going but in this time of chaos I worry we won't make it to were my mom is taking us. Secretly I'm excited because with all the bad news we received lately, we could use a vacation away. I wonder where we are going. Maybe she will take my sister and I to the olive garden, we use to play tag in the olive garden. I love going there. I bet that is where she is going to take us. Fatima had often joined us there and we built a clubhouse with sheets my Mom would bring for our picnic. Fatima made our playhouse look so cool, she was always the best at making up play houses. I can hear her laughter as she ran around the trees trying to hide from me, but I always knew were she was. The smell of fresh olives lingered in the air as the hot sun beamed on our faces.

It's very late now sorry this will be a short letter to you but I have to pack my pen and paper away with my clothes. Have a great night dear Diary.

P.s. When we get to the olive garden I'll write to you and draw a picture for you too God willing.

Maryam

October 6, 2011

Dear Diary,

Oh Diary I want to break down and cry. You will not believe me Diary if I told you. You really would not believe me. I have to tell you because I have no one else I can cry to. We did go past the olive garden but this time it did not look like the olive garden I remembered. It seems as though it had been burnt down, it smelt like smoke and dead bodies. I can't even describe to you how ugly it looked. I can only draw a picture for you at the end. It wasn't like the memories I had of it. Fatima was not laughing and the sun was not shining. I cried so hard as we past through, I sat on one of the burnt trees praying to Allah that this would all end.

Oh Diary my Mom has taken my sister and I to seek help from somewhere far. My legs hurt, I am so hungry and all I can think of is how will we make it alive. The weather is so cold at night. We are sleeping in a house that has been abandoned, probably by others who have also ran away. All day and night I hear yelling and guns firing. Diary all I have is you. I'm tired, I need to sleep because we have to walk more tomorrow.

I'll write later, hopefully.

Maryam

Syria to Turkey

October 26 2011

Dear Diary,

I am so sorry I haven't written for so long it seems. As we ran from place to place and slept in homes that were abandoned or sometimes not having a place to sleep at all, I didn't have any time to sit and write for even a minute. I am so tired of not having our home but Mom tells me it's almost over. We had to hide in a house for a day and then a bus packed with a lot of people drove to the border of Syria and Turkey where we got to cross over. As we did my mother told my sister and I that it was going to be ok now. I kept looking back wishing I could just go home, but what was our home? No father to sit with on his old chair and no family to visit, we were alone and home wasn't really a home no more as it sat in a pile of rubble. I pray my mother knows what she's doing because I have no idea. Oh the bus just stopped telling us to get off, I guess that's it we will be walking from place to place again. I am getting tired of this running, I just wish this would all be over.

I'll try to write sooner then before but if I don't ever get the chance to just know that you were my best friend dear Diary.

Bye.

Maryam

Turkey to Hungary

November 2, 2011

Dear Diary,

It seems like we have been walking for years but really it's been just a few days, I'm very grateful some people have given us rides along the way. We are about to cross into Hungary. My Mom seems to look worried that we will not have the chance to be the first ones on the busses which are supposed to be coming to pick us up. Mom said if we are to get on these buses we will be ok and safe. But she has told me this before and it was only just the beginning. I am so worried and scared we will be left behind. I can't stop my tears as I write to you, we are running from anger and hate in our homeland to watching people here arguing. There is a group of men screaming at each other to who will get on first, one group screams they should be the first. Why can't we just work together and help each other out? Oh Diary I am so worried. I don't want us to not get on but at the same time I worry for those who don't. My chest hurts and my eyes are red from crying. Here comes the buses, if I get on I will have a nap and will write to you as soon as I can.

Take care Diary, pray for us.

Maryam

<u>*Hungary to Austria*</u>

November 12, 2011

Dear Diary,

We have been in our camp which they call a refugee camp for a few days now. It's not very easy being here, there are so many of us and it's colder at night. I miss my warm bed and cozy home. Even living with my grandparents was much more better than this. My Mom is frustrated. She talks to another mother who is also trying to find refuge in Germany about what to do. We have been told we will go to a more appropriate camp once we cross from Hungary to Germany, but no one has helped us in getting there. We are in tents on the side of a train area just waiting. Layla and I haven't got to play with any toys for so long, it's like I forgot all about my toys. I think Mom is going to start walking to the border because she is becoming so impatient with waiting. I hope if she does we get to go with the other families so we aren't alone. I'm worried dear Diary. At nights I wake up from nightmares it seems to be the same one repeating every night. I keep seeing my dad's body on the ground bleeding and my Mom screaming over an over. I just don't know how much I can take. I know I have to remain hopeful but if you really knew what my thoughts were and how I feel being so lonely you wouldn't blame me for starting to lose hope. I have witnessed so much hate and anger and it seems to be getting worse by the day. I don't know how to console my mother at nights as I lay in bed I hear her cry quietly. I don't know if she's crying because of how hard it is on the ground in these camps or if she is missing my Dad. I wish I could take this all away and give her something to smile about. Oh Diary what can I do.

I should stop writing now and get some sleep, tomorrow is another day of the unknown events I will have to go through yet again.

Maryam

November 28, 2011

Dear Diary,

Mom took us by foot walking through the streets and outside the city we were in with other families. Mom didn't want to wait any long and kept saying they are prolonging us from getting to our other camp and crossing into Germany. We have to get to this camp to be able to put our asylum papers in. Mom says these papers are really important like a really important test. She said once we get them in we wait for them to mark it just like a test and either approve us or not. I'm not sure what would happen if they didn't. I mean would we have to travel back to Syria? I don't know. I guess I shouldn't worry about that yet but how can I not. I mean if we go back I'm sure we would die like the many

I've seen already. Let this be my promise to you Diary. If we are able to make it and stay in Germany and I get to go to school, I will work very hard to graduate and go to University to become a doctor. You know what I also promise, is that if I become a doctor I'll go back to Syria or go to different camps for refugees and help all those injured out. I felt useless as I seen so many in need of a doctor but could not get to one soon enough. I have to help them Diary, my chest hurts so much and I want to cry out loud but I can't. Mom and Layla are sleeping already and I am so tired too. Please pray for us Diary, and pray I don't have another nightmare again.

Write soon God willing.

Maryam

<u>Austria to Germany</u>

December 3, 2011

Dear Diary,

How are you dear Diary? I guess through all this I am still alive, so I guess that makes me well. We traveled for so long and I am so tired. Tomorrow Mom told me we will be crossing Germany. She told me that after we get there we will be able to have a normal life again and I will be able to go to school. After losing everything I guess this is good news but I worry, how will it be? Will I make new friends?

Mom told me that she doesn't want us to stand out from the rest. I don't really know what that all means but I pray to Allah that I never upset Him. I'm so confused.

I wonder if I will ever see any of my old friends again, maybe they too have ran away like us. Maybe they will go to Germany and I will get to meet them there again. I miss them all very much and it would be a dream come true to see them again, but it seems I am losing my hope in a lot of things these days. However I wonder what Germany looks like. Do you think I will like it there? I mean it's not home. Oh how I wish I could just go back home to when it was all good.

Well I better put my pen down it's late and we have a long road ahead of us tomorrow. I will write again God willing but it may take a little time.

Take care Diary.

Maryam

December 18,2011

Dear Diary,

We made it into Germany and have found a camp to stay in. After searching for a spot in the camp to stay in we finally found a room! We will have share with another family though. They have put a sheet up to divide us and like all the other camps there is no time for yourself and it's cold and dirty. My Mom has cried every night since I could remember now, I fall asleep to it but am woken up to more nightmares. It's become the normal for me now and I think Layla does too. The camp we are in is a huge building with many rooms and everyone of them is filled with people. I wonder if this is what life will be like for us? I mean is this our home forever? I thought we would get here and live in nice home and I would get to go to school again. I seen the homes in Germany in a book at my old school, I seen a country that was nice and friendly but it isn't exactly like that. Our home is not really a home and I don't think I will go to school like this. I'm so hungry I have forgotten all about eating as we traveled from country to country but now I am realizing how hungry I am. We got to have some soup and vegetables tonight which wasn't bad but really Diary I'm still hungry. Mom told me to shut off my flashlight so we don't wake up the family next to us.

Thanks Diary for being my very good friend through this journey.

Maryam

January 10, 2012

Dear Diary,

Hey Diary how are you? Sorry it took a bit to write to you but it's because there was really nothing to write about these days. I don't know the language and it smells a bit funny here. They were able to get us into some courses that will help to learn the language here. I like the classroom that the courses are in here. I wish Fatima could have seen it. I know she would have been surprised at how small our places here are! Here is nothing like back home, we had a beautiful big home and lovely garden, however the best part of being here is that I don't hear guns shooting all day. I'm getting use to it and I think I will be ok. I don't see a lot of girls my age in hijab, they dress very different from us. Mom took Layla and I to get new clothes. I don't really like wearing the new clothes because it seems tight and uncomfortable but I know it makes my mother happy. I do however love my purple hijab scarf Mom just got me. My Dad was always the one that would buy us new clothes, I really miss him. When we would get new clothes Dad would let me buy what I liked and he always made Layla and I feel like we were his favorite girls. I remember he would always have us try on the clothes and tell us how much we have grown and how much we were his blessings.

I'm going to be busy for a few months so I won't be able to write a lot. I will for sure write and let you know if anything changes or if they let me go to school. I'm very nervous that I'll never get back to school! Do you think the other girls will like me and want to be my friend if I ever get in? Mom is telling me to get to sleep as time for morning prayers is not to far away.

Good night dear Diary, thank you for always listening to me.

Maryam

June 14, 2012

Dear Diary,

It's my birthday today. I can't believe it's been one year already! This birthday is not at all like my last one, no cake or presents today for me. However, I have been working so hard at learning the language here and have mastered it. Do you know what that means? It means I'm so close to being accepted into the school here! I guess I can consider that a birthday gift.

Mom just got news that they have approved our asylum papers, this means we get to stay here in Germany and it also means we will be moving into our first home here. Oh that also means next year I will hopefully get to start school here. I'm so excited, in all this hardship there was certainly ease for me now. I can not wait to get out of this camp and finally start living a somewhat normal life. Mom has stopped crying at night and she keeps telling Layla and I that we are on the way to living a life like the others, but she always talks about Syria and what it was, and what she hopes to see one day and that is for it to go back to the old days where there was no killing. I know when it is all over my Mom would go back home in an instant. I too have my dreams, and I will work hard to achieve exactly what I want, Dad taught me this!

I got to run need to get some shut eye.

Good night Diary.

Maryam

July 3, 2012

Dear Diary,

So we finally moved into our first home and they told me I will start school next month. I am already preparing myself and Mom has tried everyday to help me improve in my reading and writing so I am ready for school. She also is excited because she did so well at learning the German language she is going to help other refugees out with how to do paperwork and just helping them along this process that we were left alone for. She's so happy these days knowing she is going to be able to provide for us a little and hopefully we won't be in this home to long before we can move to our own home. Here we share a room with another mother and her daughter. They are very nice but it would just be nice to have more privacy and my own room! I guess we will see, I have learned to take it one day at a time because things change rapidly here.

Got to go my Mom needs me to help watch Layla as she goes to get a few things from the store.

Maryam

August 25, 2012

Dear Diary,

Sorry it has taken me so long to write to you from my last letter, I have been super busy with getting ready for school. Now guess what? I am so happy because today was my very first day at my new school. This school is huge and has so many rooms with numbers on them. They even have a place to put my jacket and shoes, they call it a schließfach in German and locker in English. My teacher is super nice! We call her Ms. B. I still go with another teacher to learn how to speak their language a bit more since school is a much different setting then outside, so I'm having some issues with understanding my teacher. Here at my school they speak English too so I have to learn both of these languages and that is not easy. It is so different from my own language and I get frustrated a little, but I'm determined to master this and work hard to have my dreams come true. Anyways the first day went ok. No one really wanted to play with me at our break times and it was very boring. In class so many people asked me why I wore my hijab so I had to repeat it so many times. Some asked me to take it off or to show them my hair, while others looked at me like I was a strange dog that was walking through their halls. I hope it gets better but I guess time will tell. On a good note my Mom is making my favorite meal tonight homemade chicken shawarma and tabouli and I'm going to help make dessert which will be sesame cookies yum yum. I'll write soon.

Maryam

September 12, 2012

Dear Diary,

Schools not going very well, I mean my homework and studies are but no one wants to be my friend. I have been so bullied around by all the kids and I really don't want to go back. I wish I wasn't here no more! I know if I wasn't wearing hijab everyone would be my friend because that's all they bully me about. Why has this happen to me? Wasn't I a good Muslim? I can't talk to my Mom about this because she has also left wearing hijab. She said it was because it was to hard and she felt worried people would judge her wrong. I'm so angry! I want to cry. My mother was not just my mother she was my role model in life. I love my Mom, don't get me wrong, but she left obeying Allah. The hardest part about this is I'm also thinking this way. I'm so ashamed of my thoughts, it makes me not want to be alive no more. Life would be so much easier if I looked like them here. I just don't know what to do. I'm so confused and I have no one! Oh Diary I can't take this anymore, I know what I'm about to do and you can't talk me out of it. Sorry Diary but if I keep writing to you I'm afraid you will talk me out of this. I just can't take it no more!

Maryam

June 2, 2020

Dear Diary,

I can't believe it, I have totally forgotten to write you for years. I was so angry in my last letter to you I threw you into my closet. With school, new languages to learn, and friends to be with, I forgot all about pulling you out and writing to you dear Diary. I will try to catch you up on my life, but to be honest I remembered about you because I have no one to turn to with the situation I am in. Because I worked really hard in elementary school, plus I took extra courses on the side, this month I will graduate high school. Yeah!!! I secretly applied for a really great University in Canada. I'm so nervous and excited I really want to get in. Mom doesn't know I applied to this University, I think she will be very sad. I want to get in so bad because I really want to take their nursing program. Do you think I will get in? Oh I'm so nervous to get the letter to say I either got in or I didn't. I only have you because I can't even tell my friends or they will tell my Mom. Oh Diary so much has changed, I read my previous letters to you and can't believe what I use to be and what I have become. I want to tell you but even telling you I feel so ashamed. Oh Diary in these years I forgot about God, of course not completely but I have not been a good Muslim. I've forgotten to please Allah in so many parts of my life. To fit in I slowly removed all the practical parts of being a Muslim. I don't pray no more and I don't wear hijab. I can't believe I'm telling you this because I know I'm wrong. I really need God now to answer my prayers, but will God help me when I have forgotten Him for so long? My mother always told me Allah is Merciful but how can I be forgiven now, after so many years. I want to pray to Allah and beg Him to help me get in to this University but will He hear my cries? I don't know. If Allah helps me I will try hard to please Him. Oh my mom just called me, she said the mail is here for me. Oh, I think it's the letter from the University, please pray I get in!

Maryam

June 4, 2020

Dear Diary,

I got in!! I can't believe it, I'm beyond excited. I spent the whole night talking to my mom, she finally agreed! Can you believe it. There is some family I had never known about living there and I will need to stay with them while I'm going to the University. I can deal with that, as long as I get to go. My Mom will be helping me get passports and student visa today. I told all my friends yesterday and we got to hang out and reminisce over our futures. I'm going to miss them but I will really miss my Mom and Layla. Oh Layla she is not doing well. I hope she grows out of her rebellious years when I'm gone. I may not get to write for some time because tomorrow I'll start to pack little by little and make sure I have everything that I can take with me. We are hoping I can move there right after graduation so I can get use to the area and how to take buses there.

Got to get to bed Mom and I have a long day applying for all these documents I need to leave to peaceful Canada.

Maryam

August 2, 2020

Dear Diary,

Yesterday I landed in Canada and met my family I never knew about. They are all very nice and I share the basement with my cousin. Her name is Khadija, she is my age and they too came here as refugees not that long after we did. She is so nice and we get along very well. She reminds me of Fatima in so many ways, especially her piety. Khadija prays, even the middle of the night I see her wake up and do her prayers, she wears hijab and is ending her fasting for Ramadan tomorrow. I know if Fatima was here she would have told me about God, and she would have made me aware of my actions that was displeasing to God. Khadija didn't say a thing when she saw me with no hijab, but I felt ashamed because she is religious and I am not. She asked me to fast with her tomorrow, it's the last day of Ramadan. I told her I'll think about it, but honestly how could I fast when I don't pray or wear hijab. I remember, I promised that if I got into the University I would try to please God more. Maybe I will fast tomorrow. I mean it's one day. I need to watch a video on how to do wudu, I don't want Khadija thinking I don't know anything. It makes me nervous being around religious people and I become so sad, I remember my father when I'm here, I remember my home and I remember my ninth birthday when I prayed and wore hijab. Oh Diary, I could imagine my father being so sad that I have become this way and I could only imagine how God sees me. I have become selfish and I lost my modesty trying to fit in with my friends. I'm such a weak person, oh Diary could Allah forgive me now after so many years of forgetting Him?

It's midnight now, I see Khadija going to her prayers. I'm going to ask her to teach me about Islam as I remember only a little bit of it from when I was young. I'll ask her to teach me how to do wudu and how to pray. Maybe she will help me find God and maybe she can help answer my question I have longed to know, will Allah forgive me?

Maryam

August 12, 2020

Dear Diary,

I can not even begin to explain what it has felt like to pray again, to fast again and to cry to God all night for Him to forgive me. Khadija spent everyday since I been here helping me towards God. She told me if I repent sincerely, meaning I won't go back to my old ways and I try hard to learn and find what God wants from me, then God is very Merciful. I feel as though I have been cleansed from my past, I feel like I am fresh and that God must still care for me because I am here with Khadija at the most perfect time in my life.

Today after eight years I did my prayers in the correct way and I decided that I wanted to put on my hijab again. I just can't believe I took it off. I remember at nine I said I would never do such a thing, but then friends kept at me and it was so hard not having anyone wearing hijab at the school that I went too. Even if God forgives me I feel ashamed, there will always be pictures and memories to haunt me of my disobedience to God. I need to be strong so shaytan does not hurt my want to obey God, Khadija taught me this. I love my hijab, how I feel in it and I love praying because it's the time that I can just talk to God. I pray my homeland becomes stable and one day I could return, I pray to see my father's grave and pray he is resting in peace, I prayed for my mother who I know misses me so much and I prayed that I would be forgiven. Oh Allah how I need your forgiveness, how

Merciful you are, please have Mercy on me who had been not a very good Muslim at all.

I have one month left till University starts and I'm a little nervous.

Pray for me Diary that I do well and God will forgive me.

Maryam

September 10, 2020

Dear Diary,

So much has changed, I have decided that after the thirty-two months of schooling I will return to Syria to help them. I have changed so much in the last little while. Khadija was home-schooled and graduated high school same time as I did. She is becoming a doctor. We have talked about after she graduates her degree she will come also to Syria and we can do team work there helping those left behind. I truly believe this is my calling. I believe Allah will only be satisfied if I seek knowledge about Islam and help others too who are struggling like I did. I am also doing online classes to learn more about my religion in an Islamic institute. I pray Allah helps me to gain the knowledge about

Islam and become the best Muslim Allah wants me to be. I truly feel that with my knowledge of my beliefs and holding stronger to them then ever before and becoming a nurse everything would be perfect. I think when someone enters this type of work field, and maybe every work field one has to have a remembrance of Allah and a kind of fear so that they never do anything that would displease Allah. Also a hope so that one relies only on Allah. I have learned in these past few months that believing in Allah means obedience to Him.

Well I better go I have a lot of work to do between my nursing courses, which by the way is a lot more than I was expecting and my courses online to learn Islam more deeper. Pray for me.

Maryam

Jun 14, 2024

Dear Diary,

SubhanAllah, Glory be to Allah! I have graduated not only my nursing degree but also was able to get a bachelor's degree in Islamic studies online. I can't believe it's been so long since I wrote but life was so busy, I don't even know where the time went. These years have flown by. With Syria now cleared of all the wars and our homeland is safe I have decided to return there in the next month. I have contacted them there and was able to get granted a job at a small clinic which helps a lot of single mothers and orphans. I can not wait to go, to give something back to my homeland that I longed to visit for so long. It won't just be a visit it will be my home again. I'm so emotional I can not stop crying and thanking Allah!

Oh Diary you have helped me to have a friend to lean on in the most trying of times. You really were my only friend in this world many times. I don't want to be sad about my decision to say goodbye. I believe you should have an explanation on why it is so. I have come to realize in the last little while that I leaned too much on everyone else, even you dear Diary. So I am saying goodbye, but not because you weren't a friend throughout these years but because I want to but my words in the forms of duas and my tears on my mat in prayers. I want to lean only on our Creator, our Lord, He is the only One and there is none other than Him. I want to give my life to Him and submit every part of my being to Him. I pray on the day of resurrection dear Diary you forget the bad I did, and speak only about me in good words.

Forgive me Diary for ever wronging you.

May Allah swt help us all and grant us nearness to Him. Ameen.

Take care dear Diary, memories of you will never fade from my heart.

Don't let this be a bitter goodbye but let us rejoice for what's to come.

With much love,

Maryam

God bless you all greatly for your support in helping those in need in Syria. Your support has been appreciated, may Allah bless you greatly for your purchase of this book. Your money from this book purchase will be going to WF-Aid to help support those in need in Syria. As a special gift to all of you WF-Aid was able to receive nine pictures from the children in Syria that is attached at the end of this book.

I hope you enjoy them!

زها علوش
أعرب

مستقبلي رائدة فضاء
رسم الطالبة دعاء

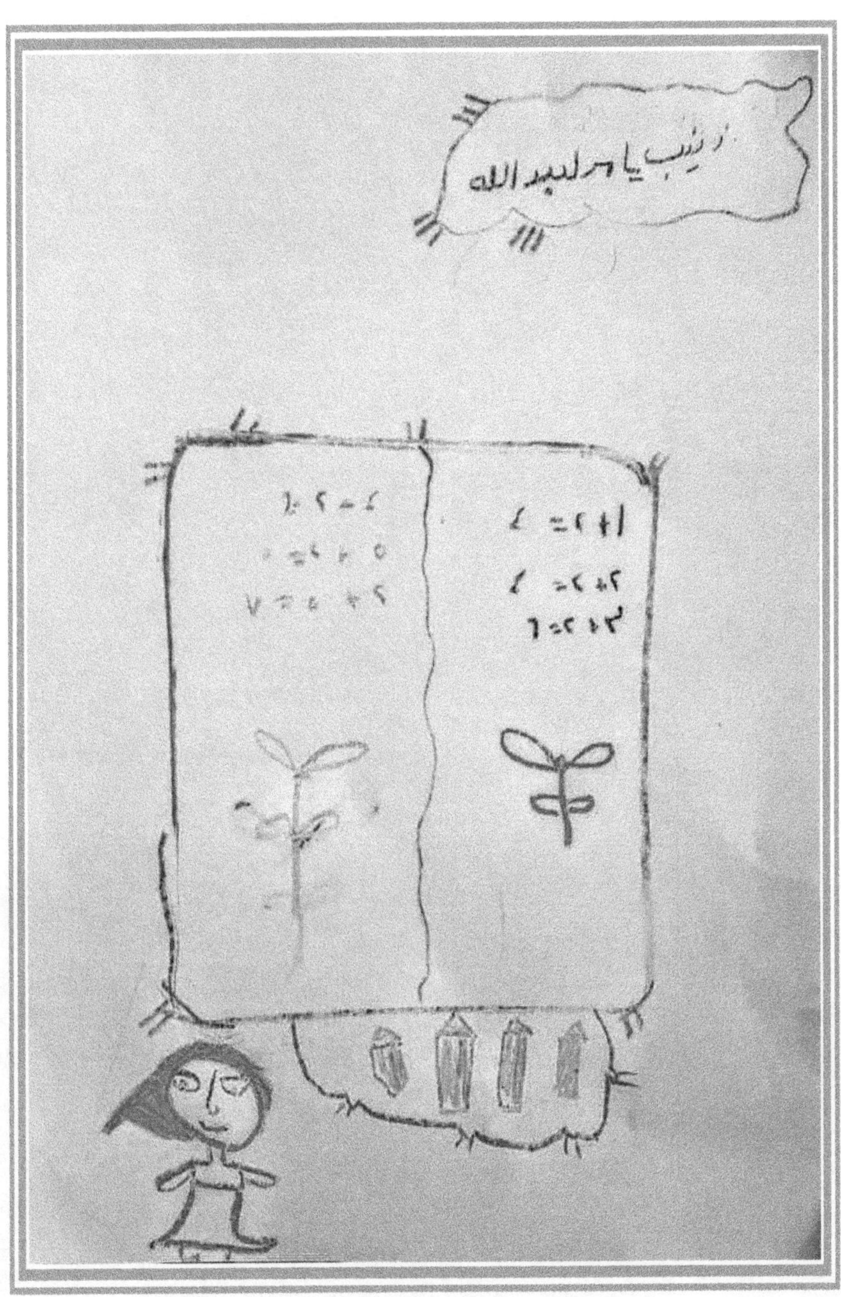
زينب ياسر عبد الله
١+١=٢
٢+٢=٤
٣+٣=٦

الثقب الأسود
مكتشفت الثقب
الأسود رقية أحمد

الاسم

بتول كشك
مستقبلي أن أكون شاعرة

الأسم: مرام

ISBN 978-1-79486-792-5
90000
9 781794 867925

www.ingramcontent.com/pod-product-compliance
Lightning Source LLC
LaVergne TN
LVHW091204080426
835509LV00006B/818

* 9 7 8 1 7 9 4 8 7 2 3 7 0 *